T0166491

Off-Season City Pipe

WORK BY

Allison Adelle Hedge Coke

COFFEE HOUSE PRESS

2005

COPYRIGHT © 2005 Allison Adelle Hedge Coke
COVER & BOOK DESIGN Linda S. Koutsky
COVER PHOTOGRAPH © Allison Adelle Hedge Coke
AUTHOR PHOTOGRAPH © Timothy Vaughan Hedge Coke

Coffee House Press books are available to the trade through our primary distributor, Consortium Book Sales & Distribution, 1045 Westgate Drive, Saint Paul, MN 55114. For personal orders, catalogs, or other information, write to: Coffee House Press, 27 North Fourth Street, Suite 400, Minneapolis, MN 55401.

Coffee House Press is a nonprofit literary publishing house. Support from private foundations, corporate giving programs, government programs, and generous individuals help make the publication of our books possible. We gratefully acknowledge their support in detail in the back of this book.

LIBRARY OF CONGRESS CATALOGING-IN-PUBLICATION DATA
Coke, Allison Hedge.
Off-season city pipe : poems / by Allison Adelle Hedge Coke.
p. cm.
ISBN-13: 978-1-56689-171-4 (alk. paper)
1. Indians of North America—Poetry. 2. Working class women—Poetry.
3. Working class—Poetry. 4. Indian women—Poetry. I. Title.
PS3553.O43660035 2005
811'.54—DC22
2004027801

FIRST EDITION | FIRST PRINTING
3 5 7 9 8 6 4 2
Printed in the United States

The making of this book has been partially supported by an individual Artist's Project Grant (formerly the Artist's Fellowship Grant) from the South Dakota Arts Council. It was further supported by a month-long residency at the MacDowell Colony for Artists and a National Endowment for the Humanities appointment at Hartwick College.

In Loving Memory of Derya Zerrin Berti

Contents

When we are forced to leave what we know as home,
we take some of the knowingness with us in spite of our need to let go.
It is this knowledge of the familiar that keeps us alive.

This book is dedicated to workers in manual arts,
to those that follow the work to survive,
to those who lost tribal status
and gained union cards,
to shanghaied people forced to labor,
to those that love the land,
to those who belong to a land faraway from foot,
to peoples in the aftermath of diaspora,
to the descendants of survivors of the long walk
to Indian Territory,
to all those who did not survive,
to those who remained in hiding,
to those relocated and dislocated peoples
finding solace in nomadic travels and kinship
in unraveling the commonality of human experience,
and the frailty of human existence,
in passion, in loss, and in yearning.

This book is my prayer for you.

For my mom and dad and all their siblings,
here and gone, and ancestors,
for my sister and brother,
my kids and theirs.

This book is my prayer for us.

For each and every hand we got along the way and
for all the hands we couldn't reach when we tried.

This book is my prayer for them, too.

"Our hands got dirty, but our hearts were clean."

Annular Eclipse, 1994

FOR DIANE

Strange light casts rain colors
on a dry but cloudy day.

    Sitting on slab steps, Rattlesnake, Montana,
        I'm thinking,
In the time Tsa la gi and Huron both
lived, as we were told,
when all men remained where they began,
pulling for The People,

today
    would have been prophetic.

Moon covering sun with full robe
midday
conception.

One star waving fringed shawl to the west
witnessing   new creation.

I'm holding a short glass of water
raised to Full Moon, Fire Circled Sun,

      for blessing.

Resonance in Motion

INSPIRED BY GREG CAJETE

In the time when they brought forth
the symbols   those syllable markings
indicating patterned speech   the old
ones   utilized in every spoken word
those characters   translating oral tongue
without need to touch our lips in our
language.   In that time when he made
these available to the people enabling
those who chose to communicate
by touching ink to page, paint to
bent fingertip to record events.
In the time   they signed away the
mother and were put to death
by the People in accordance
with written traditional law.   In that
time when people of importance
showed themselves to be of
unique character.   They gave their
lives to spare a friend or relative.
They laid down their bodies to save
their people.   In the time
when all believed the visions
and dreams of their peers.   In
the time when honesty gave birth
to mental and spiritual freedom.
In that time   we were humble,
simple as the dew on the
petal tip budding fresh from the
pastel pink and white dogwoods, as simple
as the phases of the moon,

as simple as the pass of day.
In that time we were humble,
as humble as the furry
snowshoe rabbit, as the young
doe with fawn internal,
as humble as the old ones, those robed
philosophers, the ones who
truly know   all we can ever hope
to question.   Those who were comfortable
with the flower of knowledge.
In that specific day and time,
lunar cycle,   cyclic calendar,   counted stick.
In that ever-certain moment-in-
time event, era   span   of the living   and of
the dead.   In that splitting fractional
second spanning up until those
foreign to this world appeared
that second of centuries of
millennia.   In that time,   then
we enhanced our resonance
and place, that specific center
of existence, we fasted and
retreated our projections
to visualize   clear beyond
clarity of sight   to observe
to hear the sounds   resound
above, below   and   here in this place
where we built mounds, observatories
to understand our relation
to the skies, to those heavens
spreading every night before
and above us.   Those multitudes
of lights, heavenly bodies,
seven-, eight-pointed stars, the
grandfather night sun, the

path of the spirits
those that leave here and go
onward, those that teach
us in the singing,   that vast
sky of beings   united   so intricately
to our own beings, to the
earth's beings,   to the place
from which we come   where
we find sustenance.   Those
skies we follow like charts,
or landmarks,   remembering
those suns,   the mother and
daughter,   the two that
will return one day and
the one that remains for our warmth
and for the tasseled green corn to
emerge again.   The sky that
holds both day and
night, light and dark,   the
door to the window of
Creator   and those
spirits dwelling within.
Knowing Creator
has both sides, double   time,
our Great Creator,
that giver of life,   the very
point of light matching the great
peaks of earth surrounding
the valleys, the mammoth mountains,
jagged buttes,   rolling hills we climbed to
pray.   From these we observed to center our-
selves.   In that time we believed
that which is important which
now   in this time   still continues
to exist under the surface of

this world,   the facade of this
time   which gives us sustenance
even though we often neglect
its place of honor and importance
so significant.   It allows growth
of all living beings,   continuity.
If only we work to sustain her,
together, fully to sustain ourselves.
Now the resonance appealing
to those with eyes of the swallow
the openness of the innocent,
aged infants   and little ones,
not yet jaded in humility.
This importance   now in need
of blessing,   of   spiritual tribute
as the newborn and the elder
need nurturing   to gift the
people with their wisdom and
renewal.   Now in this time
the resonance beckons   nightly
in the stars   in the moon   in the
cloudy, milky, passageway,   daily in
the sky and   in the sun   and
in the masses,   common man,
save the most jaded individual   who
returned   to a time   of violence in
heated   latitudes.   Now, in this time,
we search for what we
knew thousands of eras
ago   and   we bleed in the quest
for those flowers.   Then we
lived to one hundred seventy-five
years, we matured at around fifty-two.   Now
we die before we begin the
approach to this span   the

diseases and evils of the
foreigners,   our downfall.   Now
sclera spring rivers   cheek waterfalls
without looking to the sky
to find what appears to be out of reach   and is actually
only out of hand.   Now,
in this time,   we begin
again.   Listen, as crickets mark
these occurrences and changes   and
watch as Sun patterns
a new depth of sky.   Feel
twist in the surroundings,
be again.   Come again to the
place   from which you came to
where we do finally go,   to where I beckon
you as I have been called.
It is turning.   The dawn of
the next world approaching.
The generation coming.
It is turning.   Do you remember
they told us.   Do you remember
they brought this to us.   They
directed us to live so.   Do you
remember we are to always live
so as they instructed us.   These
voices belong to the skies,   to the
mountains.   They belong to the
past and the present,   they sing
the future.   It is in motion.

The Change

FOR THE SHARECROPPER I LEFT BEHIND IN '79

Thirteen years ago,   before bulk barns and
fifth-gear diesel tractors,   we rode royal blue tractors with
toolboxes big enough   to hold a six pack on ice.
In the one-hundred-fifteen-degree   summer
heat   with air   so thick with moisture
you drink as you breathe.
Before the year dusters sprayed
malathion over our clustered bodies,   perspiring
while we primed bottom lugs,
those ground-level leaves of tobacco,
and it clung to us with black tar so sticky we rolled
eight-inch balls off our arms at night   and
cloroxed our clothes for hours and hours.
Before we were poisoned   and
the hospital thought we had been burned in fires,
at least to the third degree,
when the raw, oozing hives that
covered ninety-eight percent of our bodies
from the sprays ordered by the FDA
and spread by   landowners,
before anyone had seen
automated machines that top and prime.
While we topped the lavender
blooms of many tiny flowers
gathered into one,   gorgeous.
By grasping hold below the petals
with our bare, calloused hands
and twisting downward, quick, hard,
only one time,   snapped them off.
Before edgers and herbicides took

what *they*   call weeds,
when we walked for days
through thirty acres   and
chopped them out with hoes.
Hoes,   made long before   from wood and steel
and sometimes (even longer ago)
from wood and deer scapula.
Before the bulk primers came
and we primed all the leaves by hand,
stooped over at the waist for the
lower ones   and   through the season
gradually   rising higher   until   we stood
and worked simultaneously,
as married to the fields as we were to each other,
carrying up to fifty pounds of fresh
leaves under each arm   and   sewing them onto
sticks four feet long on a looper
under the shade of a tin-roofed barn,   made of shingle,
and poking it up through the rafters inside
to be caught by a hanger   who
poked it up higher in the rafters   to another
who held a higher position
and   so   they filled the barn.
And the leaves hung down
like butterfly wings,   though
sometimes the color of
luna moths,   or Carolina parakeets,   when just
an hour ago   they had been
laid upon   the old wooden
cart trailers pulled behind
the orange Allis-Chalmers tractor
with huge round fenders and only
a screwdriver and salt in the toolbox.
Picked by primers   so hot
we would race through the rows

to reach the twenty-five gallon
jugs of water placed throughout
the field to encourage   and   in attempt to
satisfy our insatiable thirsts
from drinking air   which poured
through our pores without breaking
through to our need   for more
water   in the Sun.
Sun we imagined to disappear
yet respected   for growing all things on earth
when quenched with rains called forth
by our song   and drumming.
Leaves, which weeks later,   would be
taken down and the strings pulled
like string on top of a large dog food bag
and sheeted up into burlap sheets
that bundled over a hundred pounds
when we smashed down with our feet,
but gently smashing,
then thrown up high   to
a catcher   on a big clapboard trailer
pulled behind two-ton trucks and
taken to market in Fuquay-Varina
and sold to Philip Morris   and
Winston-Salem   for around   a buck a pound.
Leaves cured to a bright leaf,
a golden yellow with the strongest
aroma of tobacco barn-curing
and hand-grown quality
before the encroachment of
big business in the Reagan era
and the slow murder of method
from a hundred years before.
When the loons cried out in
laughter by the springs and

the bass popped the surface on
the pond, early on, next to
the fields, before that time
when it was unfashionable to
transplant each individual baby plant,
the infant tobacco we nurtured, to
transplant those seedlings to each hill
in the field, the space for that particular plant
and we watched   as   they would grow.
Before all of this new age, new way,
I was a sharecropper in Willow Springs, North Carolina
as were you   and we were proud to be Tsa la gi
wishing for winter   so we could make camp
at Qualla Boundary   and the Oconaluftee River
would be free of tourists and filled with snow
and those of us who held out forever
and had no CIBs would be home again
with our people, while the BIA forgot to watch.
When we still remembered before even the Europeans,
working now shoulder to shoulder with descendants
of their slaves they brought from Africa
when they sold our ancestors as slaves into the Middle East,
that then the tobacco was sacred to all of us and we
prayed whenever we smoked and
did not smoke for pleasure   and
I   was content and free.
Then they came and changed things
and you left me for a fancy white girl
and I waited on the land
until you brought her back
in that brand-new white Trans Am,
purchased from our crop,   you gave her
and left her waiting in a motel,
the nearest one was forty miles away,
but   near enough   for you

and   for her   and I knew   though
I never spoke a word to you
about it,   I knew   and I kept it to
myself   to this day   and time and
I never let on
until I left   on our anniversary.
I drove the pickup
down the dirt path   by the empty fields
and rented a shack for eighty dollars,
the one with cardboard windows
and a Gillespie house floor design,
with torn and faded floral paper on walls
and linoleum so thin over rotted board
that the floor gave if you weighed over
a hundred pounds,   I did not.
And with no running water of any kind,   or bathroom.
The one at hilltop,   where I could
see out across all the fields
and hunt for meat when I wanted
and find peace.
I heard you remarried
and went into automated farming
and kept up with America.
I watched all of you   from the hill
and I waited for the lavender blooms
to return   and when it was spring
even the blooms   had turned white.
I rolled up my bedroll,   remembering before,
when the fields were like waves on a green ocean,
and turned away,   away from the change
and corruption   of big business on small farms
of traditional agricultural people,   and sharecroppers.
Away,   so that I could always   hold this concise image
of before   that   time   and it
floods   my memory.

Off-Season

FOR FIELDWORKERS AND FRAMERS LIKE ME

Early, on grayest morning, when we
nettled deep in between rows,
tobacco and sweet potato,
both two seasons away from planting,
you reasoned I belonged there,
flowing like creek water
below our bright leaf fields,
then showing only golden stubble and root.
You said I'd never make it
swinging hammers and teething
saws for Inland Construction.
I raised my back wings, those muscles
wrought from priming rows, muscles
which cradled my ribs and sides. I
chucked tools in the flatbed, headed
north, to the city sprawled out like
scattered masonry and split rails, Raleigh,
smoked factory winds and speakeasy halls.

A white chicken fell off a Tyson rig,
just a bit ahead of me on Saunders Street.
I called her "Hooker"
from walking down the red-light street.
The Inland guy hiring was big and red,
sat behind a door laid flat for a desk on cinder block.
He chuckled much like you
at the sight of me, but the fields and breaking horses
justified my ninety pounds of lean.
Next day he had me start out on a crew full of men.
Men who'd never seen a woman work

that way in town, first
time I had a chance to operate a backhoe,
first time I got to frame, and when I swung the hammer
full leverage, three pounds drove in sixteenpennys straight.
In six weeks, I made foreman.
Just before I drove back to you.
"Hooker" almost got pecked to death
by our bantams—citified as she was.

I laid out so much money, I beat
what you pulled in for fall. We settled in
for the long freeze. You ate ridicule and haste.
We never were the same,
until spring when the fields reclaimed
us as their own and we returned
to what we both knew and belonged to.
The off-season only an off-shoot
in what we were meant to be.
You never did know this part
of what I am. Fieldworker, or framer,
I only showed you what you said I couldn't be.

Sorrel Run

FOR DAD

Sorrel-red and built to tamp devils into dust,
her withers keen,
this young mare   she challenges northers
winds her quarter-turn on a dime,
stands full-breasted, trigger-flexed,
her hinds the shape of running.

Her back flutters a deerfly, whacking the heavy air
as if it were something permeable.

My hands toss the saddle, cinch down,   and
pull me up sixteen hands, leg over
and stirruped, legs loose as if this were still
the first day on a green break lunge line.

Soon as we head out, riding open,
past thistle and gates,   she catches a gait of her own.
A strong throttled beat—deep and drumming,
my hair whipping
like a frayed flag,
all I see is the cliff edge

and her ears tilting, tilting back.   All I feel is her life-spark
charging full-center forward.   All I
know is we have about five flat minutes
on this red runaway, until it's us flying out—
and she is determined.

"*Turn her down.*"   "*Bite her ear.*"   "*Wind her
down.*"   I hear someone say inside me.   "*Turn her down.*"

My hands grip both reins and pull down,   leaning
all the way on her right side like a trick
ride at midpoint rodeo. I tug leather down to my ankle,
reach up, bite her ear, tug down, and hold   and hold   and pray
once, loud enough for prayers to carry from my mind
to the Dog Road, to Capella in Auriga,
or Deneb in Cygnus,

        and she swoops

neck over and circles tight, winds, pivots
into that particular dime turn, and every-
thing turns red as when you close
your eyes in the sun. Everything is swirling,

bent double, both of us.
We're one in the most unfavorable fashion.
Rider and horse, yes, but one and the same.

For years they said she never cut loose, or
pulled a runaway again.   But I did,
still am.   Somewhere in the circle
we traded.   I saved her; she blessed me.
She makes a great ride now and I carry out
all her plans for escape—

Breaking Horses

FOR KIM AND ROD AND ALL YOU HORSES STILL RUNNING

"This paint stud, every time I cut him loose
he starts messing around—even fresh from breeding—
biting that same mare's neck, ear, getting after her—
Maybe   'cause she's the only one
who'll put up with his shit,"
he says
      after forty straight minutes of

looking at his latest woman sideways, all the time
slitting eyes, cussing horses, slapping hindquarters,
throwing worn slack rope while she stuttered pure response
her chest cavity rippling, legs twitching, toes digging quick, hard
into dry earth

much like the stray mare's own hooves move
while the paint bites her up   and
like the mare
                        ("not bad, but nothing special, barely a quarter horse")
      she quickly half-turns
away
      quietly tossing off transpirings, head loose
searching for dignity
      still the mare's tail suddenly swishes the paint's back
and her slight hand sticks out   offering just once more,   while she's capable
some reason to let it go, head back out, forget—

Rope-burned, bottle-cut, and knuckled tight, his palm slowly opens,
extends   then, easily reaches around her waist,
pulling her close to his lean, holding on, claiming
laying certain brand by whispering,

21

"Give me some time, okeh?
    Just give me some time. Is it okeh?"

Kissing her, but keeping his back turned and his words soft and low so
    his riding buddy waiting at the gate can't see or hear.

And all she wants to do is kiss him back, lay her neck flat across his,
stand, relax, accept, yet she steps slowly back worn-down path
    allowing him range.

He's winking at his bud, smiling, shaking his head,
adjusting his braid, boots, belt loop—waving her off—
    popping open a cold one.

Looking back, the mare's fled to the hills
the stud's slobbering tank water
kicking dust, proudly quivering hard breast, tail
snorting around geldings, calling out to loose fillies
running—

    Summer heat.

Come cool weather he'll be sulking,
    she'll be shier now, a little too spooky on the right,
from full gallop in thickest woods and a lead mare's steady scold   yet
she'll turn around, and not because she wants to,
    but because horse dreams and sudden wind compel her,
tell her what he needs, and

because her simple mare sense
    tells her she's already his
        there is nothing else she can do.

But she's a dun, he's used to bays.
And the season's made him colder, tougher, mean

and once he's confident he could,
    once he's sure she'll stand with him,
he'll flee, kicking and biting on his way out, chasing a young bay filly
       still fat from lack of sense, and all the same old
    swaybacked mares stubbornly willing to share.

She shows up now and then
but each time he cuts loose, messes around,
    gets after her—

Still, you'll see her sometimes peeking over the hill, standing alone,
or out with last year's colt,   avoiding scorn and bite,
mixing uneasily with the herd
    but only when they need her or she needs survival warmth
and even then they shun her   to attract his favor.

She takes it, she knows there's nothing else they know
    (she's a stray, a barely quarter horse, but still a mare)
       it's all she knows too.

Somewhere surrounded only by iced fence and steep drift.
No matter what she wants, she'll go down
    much too early this year
       steaming fresh snow
      due to the forty-three-below windchill, lack of shelter, lack of hay,
      old whip wounds, a wintering sickness,
rifting spirit and perhaps
         just too much heart to weather
           this particular cold.

Over and over she'll swing her head up hard,
throwing herself   trying to stand
       and all the time it's snowing—

He'll be too busy to notice, sulking, showing off,
    eying the herd,
or even if he does, he'll bite
                    get after her—

So it is with horses.

Red Stone Panther

FOR TRAVIS

The first time he saw a strand, malamute fur,
he thought it was a miniature porcupine quill.
Once he said this, we could all see the quill—translucent white to
    black point.

By the time he was one,
his eyes peeked through cat-claw slits
poked in soft, tawny skin
filled with toddler pudge and grins.
They melted away everyday danger
like it was copper in campfire.

His nose still so tiny it boasted no hint
of mountainous bridge from his grandfather
and grandfathers before him.

This is how he was when he called forth his own name.
This is how he was prancing

into the wood-walled room by rock fireplace.
Leaping   onto its stone perch.
Just far enough away from flame to   stretch
rubbing his belly and smiling so great
his cheeks filled with heat
glowing red as hot stones behind him.

Snapping his tongue on extra-thick frenum
that out of our whole bunch only he has.

His eyes peeked and flicked invocation.
Bristling attention up our backs uttering,

    "I am Red Stone Panther"

    in English, and in Indian.

And he was.
    We could all see it was obvious, this is who he was.

Everybody said he was tired of waiting
and didn't want to be just a baby, now that he was one.

His black hair slickened to the top of his whirling crown,
twisting into baby braids
        down his neck.
            Stretching into his own as panthers do.

This is who he remains.
This is who he is   leaping
across sunbaked stone ledges into our world, claiming it for his own.

Putting Up Beans

FOR HAZEL AND DEJA

My cotton-covered lap aproned for canning,
summers ago, I snapped green beans for an old lady.
Green beans far from French-styled,
not even French Canadian,
more Huron I suppose, Tsa la gi on the southern side.
Holding hard with indexes, thumbs, double-handed
popping apart plump green strings
fresh from leafy hills in the fields.
Bristling with bees and dirt wasps.
Slightly rubbery, slightly sweet
enough bushel baskets to put away winter hunger
for about another year.

I remember the first time I canned in the barns,
tobacco barn burners gassed up blue,
I filled four steel washtubs with seventy pint jars each—
forty if they were quart-sized Masons.
The barn itself layered in rafters
for hanging sticks
filled with great leaves of tobacco, green as beans.
Though soon to be gold and brown-cured.
Now nowhere near Winston or Salems.
Not even close to American Spirit.
More likely Bull Durham and Drum.

Full flavor sticks hung all through the entire shingle barn,
above my head where I set gas to boil beans and
waited outside underneath the tin shade
resting on poles which were only sideways logs.

A wasp landed near my shoulder
and died.
Maybe it got cured inside the loft.
It was huge, black, hard, and shiny, so
large the only dime in my pocket
barely marked its half trunk.

I remember ant lions tossing dust
up over the dead wasp
like a funeral.

And the funeral for the grandma down the road

how she'd spent so much time making this apron
I remember on my lap.
In a time where women don't wear
aprons much anymore.

Packin' Four Corner Nabs

FOR ALL THE CRACKER-PACKIN' GIRLS

fourteen, I'm packin' crates
Fairmont Foods—Cary, NC
only mixed-blood "Indian-blonde" girl around
only factory workside worker not black
all of us under white Super's thumb

tho when shop stewards hound dues
I don't know what's what
thinkin' this work here
is dues enough
what's a union do for me?

Sadie, she took my arm, said,
"Listen, you stick close to me
when you go out back,
they're gonna get ya."
Me, I follow

suit down, shower up
snack bar and closing

fourteen, I'm still wild yet
don't know enough to be scared
so I never am
that's how I got these scars here.
Anyway, I follow Sadie

she's about fifty
and weighs five times that
just before the door she

grabs a hunk o' rebar
and latches my hand

we start out back
light up a Camel straight
look left, *there's about twenty,*
eyes rebound right, *twenty count more,*
they semicircle in

memory rings—I hear my dad's voice advising me 'bout
        fightin' white girls
"Circle 'em, they're easier to pick off"

Sadie swings the rebar
and calls 'em all on down
warning, "Touch one corn silk
on this girl's head and
I'll kill ya'. I will, too."

Her eyes round and circle wild
her big bosom heaves breath
she swings round and wide
hoping for reason to let out some rising steam

half a century's factory work
crackers, all those crackers
four corner nabs under her belt
500 gallon vats—peanut butter
stink so strong the smell

lasts a lifetime and more
crackers flying by 'bout ninety miles per

pull and pack ten-
thirty, if you're a stacker

pull and pack ten filled and
wrapped on belt conveyors
drop in cardboard containers

pull ten more
till ten times ten makes
one hundred count boxes—
Austin Foods—all the scrambled ones
go to feed dog, or hogs

somewhere, they say,
somewhere far, far, away

lookin' at Sadie swing rebar
you know she's packed plenty
I wish I was packin' more 'n fists
studying Sadie I surmise
her punch'd be good as my drop cut

on the so-white preacher's daughter's nose
when she called me a heathen
I was proud of breakin' it in one jab but
my dad said I maybe just
proved her right

Hell, I didn't even know what a heathen was
guess this union thing must
be like a club for preacher's daughters
I decide and slide
shuffle step slide
in to back up Sadie's swings

swing low, swing high, swing 'round and back

never had an older woman
fend for me before
defended plenty though
guess it's fair in all
Union guys they

just pull in and pull back
like a boxer afraid to land
case he might get landed on
Sadie is so big to me
she's the midnight blue of sky

just swings and swings with fear of God
human pendulum momentum
strutting her stuff through the crowd
straightening 'em out like scolding babies
"Didn't your mama hold you?"

"What you big men wanna beat
a tiny girl like this for?"

I look down my upper arms
fully bulged from field work—
furrows and packin' crate and
concrete block—
heavy work side I live

they just don't fit my build
so I look like a monkey
when I look in mirrors
big muscular arms and back on
a skinny little frame

kinda wiry, funny, even to me
the biceps aren't tiny, I think

and pull back my jacket
to show 'em off
let 'em ripple with blood pumping

never did know when to be scared
even when I was really shy

Sadie steps through
Austin Food's finest forty
like walkin' water, she steps
I walk right on by behind her
they begin shuffling, shuffling

away at her words and
at the Super's floodlights

now circling us and flashin'
like a prison yard
counter escape
warden Super packin' something else
we're past and out

I look at Sadie
she whispers low, only to me,
"Better get them dues paid.
Next check, okeh?"
I nod, duck out the lot

hitch a semi home down
highway 50   smellin' like crackers
and peanut butter from packin' four corner nabs
even after the shower down
spot a Teamster card on the visor

The Dove

FOR JOY

A dove must've died here—
hurled feathers swirl in
    sidewalk joints,
grey on gray,
a seizure of wind sends them spiraling
like lace curtains plastered
    onto building brick—

back toward the Amtrak in Albany.
The open window has haunted
trainloads for decades.
Faces steamed into glass from passengers
peering so close their live breath left

despair and dreams.
Faces robbed of peace, stretched by desperation,
displaced and discarded faces, longing—
on the same fifty-year-old
    forties train I rode here on.

A moment ago a blind lady entered
the intersection to my left,
saying, "Trapped birds they are.
    Why can't they just use buzzers like in Watertown?
    These signals sound like trapped birds."

I feel myself fighting every day,
straining to remain feathered.

Gently I lift my shoulders,
elbows invert, wings taper down.
My face hardens and beat pelts.
My toes grow long and claw over
    sidewalk lines and cracks

glimpsing
    underneath the city swirling.

#4 Southwest Chief/L.A. Central

FOR DERYA AND HEID

The sheen of incandescent lamppost light travels this rail,
up ahead the Conductor
reminds us, "if there's anything
we can do to make your trip 'worthless' just let us know"
and no one cracks a smile.

This Amtrak car glides between
concrete pillars wrapped with steel for quake protection.
Projects plastered in graffiti by day now sink into 9:00 p.m. comfortable—
this time of night you'd think they were condos

if you rode this rail for the first time.

What I see is concertina riding chain-link fence tops—
as if there is an escape attempt due any moment.

Then, somehow, I see myself in the window. Not a reflection
but an actual replica looking back at me and at the glare,
over further than a bounce of light could flash, where
planes coming in to land look like falling stars,

and I'm taking my mother to the asylum in my memory.
I can still hear her saying, "Bad, bad girl." and "Look
at the pretty stars and Christmas lights," sometime late July.

L.A. River on my left, tonight there's water more than trickle down.
Along the concrete banks where someone wrote out "RECKLESS"

a concrete mixer is parked right by the river and rail,
and one single truck has its lights on bright.

By morning, jump starts will cardiac it back to life.

My gut aches. The whole world's in a window at Fullerton and
through arches, past electric globes, it spins
high over a Pepsi machine on the floor far below.

Bad, bad girl. Look at the pretty stars and Christmas lights.

Baggage

FOR PUMPKIN

We watched grocery rows
through an iron grate,
strangers' hatted heads
below our feet and floor.

In the small-town apartment
straddling the general store
we spent days and nights
pretending to be spies.

My sister and I
still young enough
        to carry.

We were
carried in with
a banded wheat-colored suitcase,
its sides blackened
from radiator burns,

Our crumpled cotton shifts
And wax crayons
Tucked inside.

Attached to the handles were
        fluttering tags,
the names
of those who dropped
        us here
                and left.

Each time the customers
strode aisles below
they might have been walking
softly lit halls between
psychiatrists and guards—my

daddy visitor, mama patient,
in Dix Asylum.

Self-Immolation

FOR WALTER

His Levis laced with gasoline
so thick wet legs became funnels.
No, wicks, in a holocaust.
Skin turning into hard ash.

"Roll me in a blanket"
"Roll me in a blanket"

Screams from the burning board floor.

Windows blown out.
Doors blown off.
Flames blowing, blowing,

"Roll me in a blanket"

I threw one to my dad.
We smothered charred legs.
We smothered the entire room:
walls, doors, window frames,
bed, and bike

dirt bike, 175 Yamaha.
He was cleaning it with gas
and stealing one of my smokes,
a Winston filter.

I peeled his pants.
The meat came with the denim.
We placed him in ice water,
bones exposed,
muscles barely hanging.

The only time he ever said,
    "I love you"
    "I'm sorry for all the
       things I've done."

I believe it now,
twenty-two years later.

The smoked venetian blinds
shook in the wind like breastplates.
Scorched ticks swollen up like grapes
full of blood
climbed the cheap paneling
trying to escape.

Like me, he'd tried to take
       his life.
Like me, we both survived.

Wachovia Wilds

FOR LITTLE BROTHER

Green-eyed, mixed-blood
thirteen-year-old NC boy
holds up the Wachovia Savings and Loan
with his plum jam finger.
Greenbacks flow from teller
to brown paper sack.
Everybody else is facedown for 360°.
He knows they're trembling, shaking like
he does when Mama's lecturing
the lightbulb
all through the night. They're
quivering from pressure on
points unknown and underdeveloped.

He knows it's all going smoothly.

Two older boys guardpost the door.
He backs out, ducks
and tucks for cover, running to catch
the yellow and black Impala
as it makes the block with three other
Hanes-faced boys.
Soon they all lay sprawled out in Motel 6
covered with U.S. currency, small bills and large.

They never were picky kids.

Green-eyed boy, he's stuffing his pockets full
swearing, "Ain't gonna work my ass off
and be stuck in steel toes like my old man, 'cause
there's a foosball parlor in Virginia with my
name written all over."
Right outside, the county's finest
outline clear shots on each figure fingering dough.
Sheriff's softly singing:

"In the sweet by and by . . . "

This He Learned
by Being American

FOR WALTER

He called me a "welfare slut" and
I never spoke to him again.

This he learned by being American
    by trying to be white.

I hung up the phone,
diapered my youngest,
and got ready for school and work.

The food stamps burned my fingers
in Safeway on the way home.
That night felt especially heavy
wondering where the harlot lay.

I questioned my abstinence
as if a name pushed on me
would materialize into something promiscuous.

I questioned my worth.

This he learned by being American.

Sleeping in a Hundred-Year-Gone Brothel

FOR THE GHOSTS OF WORK PAST

Four hours before dawn
raises the lid above this building, #226,
four ladies circle
a service table
that in daylight does not exist.
    Buttoned and laced
    leather boots   leggings
    and corsets binding white flesh.

I wonder why they have come.
Why they show themselves this way.
Watching me, in my gown, twist and turn all night
must have been familiar.
All night turning an attraction of its own.

We are both restless,
    but not   alike.

They raise their tea and whiskey,
fan their penciled lips
and reach toward my shallow breathing.

They want something
                  live.

I smell strong burlesque
perfume   two-dollar bourbon,
stale cigarettes, and heavy sweat.

Their faces twist,
       contort,
           transform,
to wicked, wrinkled, atrophy.
They pull and suck and force themselves on me.
I am paralyzed from the ears down,
but feel my spirit
    falling   into grey brothel rooms, into older nights,
death and slickly polished nails.   Falling into corset laces.

    My mind becomes a song
    in place of my frozen lips.
    Over here, the people are happy.   *Over here, the People.*

Street Confetti

FOR STEPHANIE

Right across Turk Street, south side intersection Hyde,
in the tenement where 911 won't summon up a blue,
a man beats his woman,
the twentieth time or more, their kids bawling.
Over here, in this flat up on the third,
above blazing red neon signs highlighting
the *Triple Deuce Club* low below, I listen while
wired white hippies move furniture across checkered tiles
other side my sister's arched plaster ceiling till way past 3 a.m.
Shuffling with a sofa as if rearranging the heavens in my mind.

Me, I sleep. Or try to. Nothing else I can do.
Each day I slip off and out looking for work, gliding into the
Streets of San Francisco
winding, curving, like turbulence.
Daybreak brings sweet Cambodian street children out
into a Feinstein-era playground,
still filled with hypes, winos, yellow-green from the night before,
still smelling like piss and lizard.

These kids though, they climb atop steel swing-set bars,
fifteen, twenty feet high,
as if they're walking joint lines in concrete.
Easy balance, Mohawk grace.
Their sisters provoke a paper war in the street,
          closed-off   block party.
     Paper flying by, I
catch a piece, fold it origamically, create
a mock financial pyramid, toss it back,
watch little girls with black shiny ponytails make confetti
for this ongoing ticker-tape parade,
right across Turk Street, intersection Hyde.

Eternity Safeway

FOR VAUGHAN

Curses whisper from
Somewhere beyond our peripheral vision.
Parking lot, Safeway.
    safe way
Leaning back
my light brown boy says,
"Mom, there's no one there."

The curses continue,
not from human lips,
at least not those in the here and now, but
someone's on the other side.
    over *there.*

One who walked this gray Safeway plaza
a million times or more.
One who still tries to catch the glass auto-door
at precise moments to mingle with the living,
or at least those convinced they are.
Slipping into box boy mania,
aisles and aisles dwindle
to checkered cashiers,
the lowest-paid public performers.
Waitresses barely beat 'em out by tips.
Only tip number three gal ever received was to bundle up,
the front moving in quicker than predicted.

Box boys bring oxygen tank
for lady senior,
as if it were a box of Rice Krispies.

The tank's connecting blue plastic hose is
Lady Grey Hair's extended visa to
Planet Earth.
She climbs into silver taxi.
Her driver pulls away.

Hearing vulgar whispers, my mind
Brings back the bag lady next to dumpster,
late last summer,
who claimed her son would
come back

any day.
He didn't really mean to leave her in the
city
all
alone.

Mornings my hands passed oranges and sandwiches
into her crab cage palms
two times a week. And I remember

that other one,
the apple-dried older man
who talked out loud though
no one understood.
He was Indian, like a lot of us,
but we didn't know what tribe,
what *dialect*, he was.
He couldn't trust us to take him away from the granite curb.
Someone had pushed him out a car door where he still waited.
As if whoever dumped him like a box of styrofoam
would return,   take him home.

Government Relocation Program victim?
No one really knew.
We gave him sandwiches, sardines and mayonnaise.
My kids rolled him an old wool blanket.
Over the years he went from limp
to cane
to walker,
some Skins got him a nice one
from St. Vincent de Paul.
Then some rank skinheads trashed his aluminum aid,   they
got him drunk
        holding back his head.

He must have been close to ninety
when he disappeared.
We asked everyone for miles an' miles,
at corner stores,
on curbs,
sidewalks,
streets,
all over Indian town,
no one ever knew
where he went,
who abducted him this time.

If he lived and breathed.

Or, died alone
picked up by street sweepers
brushing up loose leaf.

Leaning back
hearing whispers
my light brown boy says,
"Mom,

there's no one there.
Can you hear cussing?"
I smile,
rub his shoulders,
"I know, kinda scary, huh?"
He blinks and listens.

City Pipe

FOR DERYA

I'm trailing these streetsides, picking fruit
hear a man scream from the gully:

*Dumpster flames dilate my eyes
as quickly as licorice and Tabasco awaken my belly.*

*It is a conspiracy,
this raspy conjuring.*

*I furnish soup cans for spiders,
guilty of fulfillment and praise.*

*Their tongueless jaws size up the labels like stamen
and devour plush minerals, vitamins c and a.*

*As punishment for my kindness
I am cast away like roadkill,*

*in this seedy city, laid off from
City Pipe.*

*Euro-assailant, Manifest Destiny, plantation and miner reasoning,
greed as justice, as "claiming territory," of these Ortiz sings.*

*Boom, boom, boom!
Forge ahead!*

*Romantic flicker the stacks of persimmons
wherever bridges conquer Bakersfield.*

Just one more field to pick.

Valencia St., Mission District

FOR D.D.

I can't edge out the eyes, hollow coffins,
blinded, can't edge out steel needles,
maybe cloroxed, maybe not, scraped on matchbooks,
finely honed, as if sharpening a stone,

I can't dodge the heat rush, the blood and boil,
in my elbow pits, my memory banks,
the memory of retching. Rot and gut.
But it's not me this time.

Still a silver sliver spike
spies on me, like a periscope, code name: Blues,
persistent from another time, a measure—metronome,
touching time. And time touches me the way

a latex glove taps his brown cheek.
The patrolman pushes a slightly turning Aztec angled jaw.
I'm remembering my own jaw cop-slapped decades back.
Poor guy, I mutter to myself.

All the while I'm walking my today's ways, teaching dignity,
working poetry into Chemical Dependency exercise
juvenile facility, literary addiction
and, man, I just want to see him rise. Just stand up.

Poor guy. I'm looking back.   Poor guy.   And I do need him to rise
need him to stand, regain Houdini mentality to stand,
"get up on your feet now, rise, take your stand. . . .   Let it fly.
This time. Let it fly. Let it fly. Let it sail."

Voucher, Voucher

FOR TRAVIS & VAUGHAN

Suds and Duds Missoula
Salvation laundry voucher
handles three loads per
call over the operator
just as he said and
pour a capful of soap from the
coffee can for voucher use
he says, Did you touch this!
more demand than question
You, you don't touch anything here!
That's what I'm standing here for.
gives me the scold like I'm
twenty years ago and sleeping in here or something

already had confrontation
coming through the door
he says, What are you in for?
as if he can't see the baskets and duffel I'm dragging
hand him the voucher some Red Cross man gave me
he looks at it says, what about the steward
See, here it says he signs here . . .
oh, he signed already
Well . . .
Who is going to vouch for this
voucher? As if he really needs to know.
I tell him just to get it over
he asked me back what I just said
He's back at the plant, huh?
looks me over saying Oh.
that's all just Oh. like it dumb-

founded him. Oh.
the second time approval
That's okeh load 'em in
14, 15, 16 and call me when you need
to start 'em up . . .

soon as I unload to dry
he's wiping down the machine
our clothes were in
like we're contaminated just cause
we had a voucher

my son he moves a chair
to see TV a little better
operator scolds him too
but my boy looks at me rolling
eyes and grins a zipper edge

big, big white man
pure pasty
glasses, neatly trimmed beard
trophy buck on T-shirt worn Levis
handles hanging way over
gut sticking out under deer's tongue
keychain dangling off belt loop
Are these guys born with keys
hanging off their diapers, or what?
he bangs on vending
till the chips fall
but if anybody else nudges it
it's a fine of twenty-five

First Officer, Commander Riker
Star Trek above our heads
this guy he's got the same beard as
the coin-op operator
but much more intelligence in his eyes

Operator smokes
lets ash fall to floor
and watches to insure
we don't do the same
good thing I'm too broke to smoke
and gave it up for coming autumn

all I want is this Pulitzer
with my name on it and all
I want is to live and help others live
better than I have
I'm writing, dreaming 'bout the prize
I know it's mine
somewhere in here I know
it is already just
they don't see it
looking past these eyes
condemning me bad as when
I was thirteen and sleeping coin-
ops   twenty-two years ago

trashy white blondes, peroxided ones
smoke and giggle sentiments to
the teenage boys being cool

doing laundry maybe 1st
year college or 1st year away
from home   too sleek to be on
the street   trashy by choice
rebelling mainstream mama and daddy
think they're better than that

girl, that Pulitzer is all that's pulling me through

Allen Ginsberg Comments on Joe Hipp, 1994

FOR THE NORTHERN PLAINS INTERTRIBAL
POETRY BOUT BUNCH

I have met the greatest fists of our time.

I saw the best fists of my generation bounce off
*the biggest Browning boxer—*THE BOSS*—the greatest*
I have ever seen. I have been to Montana myself
Once read for Writer's Voice, YMCA,
in Billings and on Crow, and I have to say
this day stands out like no other . . .

USA Channel 24 Missoula.
Should have been a smoker.
Joe "The Boss" Hipp vs. Jose "El Niño" Ribalta,
late night USA TV.
It should have been great
blasting my yard-sale Sony
pumping fibervision for pay.
I must've dozed deep, work spent, my eyes rapid rabbits
like those punches kicking the brains outta skulls.
Joe Hipp, big as ever, that undeniable Indian build.
What a fight! What a fighter.
Should've been smoke for me to curl.

Whom pound?
He pound him!
Whom pound?
He pound him!
Whom pound?
He pound him!

Whom pound?
He pound him!

Should've been a smoker,
I say and turn over other side.
Where's Joe? Where's our Indian hope? Our hero.
We all need Joe, just like we needed Plunkett
in L.A. Raiders 1988. Fifty thousand people calling:
Plunkett, Plunkett, Plunkett!
Dropped in my stadium dime deliberately
acknowledging my dad, "yes, yes, it does feel great!"

Hiway Posey
Right now they're trying to take
the Indian territories
          away near Hopiland.
Subdivisions,   mineral rights—
          the last stand
newspapers claim we'll murder them
like 100,000,000 bison—
Look it's a smokestack smoker
     bombshells crash on flesh
"I won't like to die
          a man   I ain't about to crawl."

Can't stand
Can't stand

Don't smoke
don't smoke
don't smoke
Don't smoke
Don't smoke
don't smoke
don't smoke
Don't smoke

The body's a big beast
    The mind gets confused
Soft shoe dancing on the moon
    Hipp, Hipp, Hipp!

Can't stand
Can't stand

Only the eye flickering carcass

returns me to the ring.
Hey, who is Greg Kinnear? Where's Joe?
What's Allen on for? We got the right channel or what?

Don't smoke
Don't smoke
Don't smoke

El Niño K-O'd in the 2nd I awoke.
Yeah, Boss, you got smoke.

A White Lady Speaks

FOR BETTY FROM THE AMTRAK EMPIRE

A white lady speaks
 and she tells

that she
 was an Indian once, too.
That she dreamed
 she fell off a cliff
and knew

and she asks me for a cigarette

and she tells that she
 played the Indian

while her brothers
 played cowboys

she reaches into sequinned blouse,
 studded purse

and she asks me for a light

and she tells that her
 cousin also works at

an Indian school so
 he is an Indian, too
  in a way

and she asks me for a pen

and she tells that she's
    moving to a reservation

to teach the Indians
    about the environment

and she asks me for some paper

and she tells that her
    thesis will be on

Indians so she wants a book list
and she asks me to write her one

she says she's already read
    Medicine Woman and
    Jaguar Woman so
not to bother with those two

and she tells that she
    doesn't believe in being

angry, that she believes
    in peace

and she asks me not to write
    down any political books

and she tells that if her
    kids were Indian she

would raise them into
    medicine men and women

and she asks if I know Lynn Andrews

and she tells that she's
    had sex with several

Indian men and had that
    savage love she needs to
        make her medicine babies

and she asks if I have kids

and she tells that she
    wants to teach Indian

kids about their
    heritage

and she asks if she could
    see my kids sometime

and she tells that she
    loves the way the

ceremonies speak to
    her, the ones she reads about
        or sits in on

and loves the holy people
    like Harley Fast Buck
    and Agnes Chuckling Cow

and she asks if I am related
    to anyone like that

and she tells that she
　　doesn't have to worry

about her ancestors
　　because they were
nowhere near Wounded
　　Knee, or Custer's Last Stand

and she asks if mine were

and she tells that she
　　has so much to give

to Indian people, especially
　　old people—"the ones who don't know anything"

and
　　she asks
　　　　for another

　　　　　　smoke

Wheat

FOR MOM

I stand behind a window
where lovers once built the only walls
still standing.   A window.

There are no wheat fields
this close to the Pacific blue.

Though I toss live seed in the brick-lined
geranium and cannas beds   each time
I winnow hulls from the bird feeder,
no tempest tousles its head toward
these grey steps, screened door.

Though there is seldom a time
I am without wheat.

Since childhood, it's been there—amber,
something straight
filling fields, reaping full futures,
flaxen. Since childhood,
shaking rustles,
seeds my mind with
gold and beige,   with near colors,
void of closure, so

somewhere, in me, in the field fanning
outside this sashed and latex-painted window
wind patterns shaft and grain into full run.

Pulp and Thick Skin

FOR DIANE, MARGARITA, AND JUAN FELIPE

The desire so strong your steps quicken
back to the house.

You   don't even want   to peel it, you grab
the big butcher knife   over the breadboard and
slice   it in half like a grapefruit
each section firm and bright.
A sugar spoon lifts the first bite separating
pulp and thick skin,   with this taste
is knowledge.

Heading out back
through rain-soaked grass, brown mud,

the orange trees drenched, bloom again.
little white blooms,   almost like honeysuckles
with the thickness of lilies,
freshly clustered amid grove green leaves.
Leaves so thick they split when   you fold them double.
Orange trees filled with blooms and green fruit
when just last week   you could stand a field away
and witness ripening.

Everything's so wet and cool, the ground gives
with each step, grasses plastering canvas shoes.
If you walk around a tree slowly,   looking deep into
hidden limbs,   huge fruit so ready to squeeze, to be
devoured, hangs steady inviting plucks.

Your arm slides in the wet, wet tree.
Rain still alive within its branches,
covering your arm and hand,   splashing you with morning.
Your arm glides in and picks the nearest one, stealing
fresh crispness for the table.

If you grew up like me, you find yourself back in time
picking fruit in the fields,   remember.

Waking to pick in wet groves each morning.   Sacks on your
waist and shoulder, crates, five gallon buckets below.   Filling huge
crates stacked in rows and trucked off to Minute Maid
or Sunkist. But right now it's the taste
you need. The wet, sweet-sour citrus.

Casting Vessel

FOR MARY, SARAH, AND SAM,
AND EVERYONE STILL CASTING

Pamlico
Sound
flamingos,
hot pink
gentle grace   braced
on one leg
against
feathered snow,
swans wearing
black masks.
Spanish moss hanging,
netting tall
trees surrounded
by kudzu,
greenest vines creeping,
as we net
jumping mullet
and shrimp,
drift nets
across the bank
on the Atlantic,
the Outer Banks
of Carolinas,
highest corner
of Bermuda's
Triangle,
up past Emerald Isle.
The voices
of a thousand
waterfowl

carry our boat
with waving motion
back to you.
We gig flounder
and scoop up
live scallops,
with their
iridescent rim
of blue eyes shining
from the very
edge of protection.
Not a crease
on the water,
the breeze remains
among the treetops
kissing fluffs
of swan clouds
slipping from
the blue, blue
sound of sky
above   dotted
by   wing,
goose and
diving ducks,
those who
pierce the
crest of waves
to fish with
skill of pelicans   by
the sound of
sky and sea
surrounding   and
holding all this
sacred blue bowl
of intricate   design.

Waiting for the Last Lunar Eclipse, 2004

FOR ALL THE HOMO FLORESIENSIS

I dreamed of a sudden eclipse
revealing unexpected stars
causing me to shift in my sleep,

remember mounds assembled,

basketful by basketful—the building.
Various earths carefully compiled
commemorating dead immortal

underneath compelling skies.

A woman peeling slivers
from a great ball
hanging loose leavings
like locust leaf—silver.

Then stars filled sky—radiant.

While earth wrapped moon in rose
I imagined night briefly breaking
light barriers like pulses, in other

daytimes, somewhere far beyond.

Here in the muck of morning,
where gray slates sky
and drizzle threatens,
Oneonta, New York,

a star, or two, may hover blind.

Constantly preparing plenty
wholly pondering day,
hoping to light the world like us,
and we in welcome wait.

Acknowledgments

Appreciation for past and continual support and inspiration from: Derya Berti, Diane and Skuya Zephier, Kim Shuck, Janelle Swallow Price, Marsha Stands, Faith & Susan Two Eagle, Eleanor Weston, Crystal Bush, Sandy Hinkle, Marilyn Lonehill-Meier, Molly Bigknife & Gino Antonio, Martin Brady, Martina and Angel Old Horse, Pte Sa Tokahe Win "Sawee" Frank, Adam George Two Eagle Jr., and the twins: Edward and Edwin Two Eagle;

all the people who hosted me during residencies, and all the people who provided me work and past literary and professional support, including: Ruth Brennen, Val Fox, Janet Brown, Michael Pangburn, Lori Frush, Susan Stoneback, Deb Klebanoff, Shari Kosel, Pat Boyd, Cynthia Tjaden, Karen Walker, Mary Halseth, Bill & Ann Thompson, Susan Bernardin, Diane Glancy, Bob Bensen, Phil Young, Arthur Sze, Jon Davis, Anne Waldman, Carol Lee Sanchez, Spencer and Lauren Werth, Ellen Arnold, Joy Harjo, Betty Holyan, Heid Erdrich, Juan Felipe Herrera, and Margarita Luna Robles;

all the activists who joined me in bringing mentorship and literary arts to incarcerated children, with special emphasis on incarcerated Native youth, including: Gino Antonio, Cris Apache, Neilwood Begay, Kimberly Blaeser, Win Blevins, Randi Bomar, James Blue Wolf, Susan Campbell, Christina Castro, Heid Erdrich, David Evans, Diane Glancy, Juan Felipe Herrera, Barbara Helen Hill, Arlene Hirschfelder, Janet McAdams, P. F. Molin, Irvin Morris, Mark Nowak, Jackie Old Coyote, John-Carlos Perea, Nita and Harry Pahdopony, Larry Pringle, Suzanne Rancourt, Margarita Luna Robles, Kim Roppolo, Steve Russell, Kate Shanley, Kim Shuck, James Stevens, Gene Thin Elk, Martha Ture, Anne Waters, Jody Willett, Norma and Jerry Wilson, and Chuck Woodard.

My students, from three to ninety-three;

Travis,
Vaughan, Mary, Hazel, and Deja

This book is for you.

In memory of Auntie Rose, Uncle Bud, Cousin Bernice, Cheryl, Derya Zerrin Arabas Berti, and great heroes: Brownie McGhee and Ray Charles;

and with prayer for all those affected by the trauma of war and hatred, for those who've lost loved ones, for those workers and volunteers who fought and fight to save lives, for those displaced and disemployed workers, for those who work for peace and better ways, and with great peaceful prayers for those of us who have few living relations left here on Earth to walk with still. Let us walk fully, without shame or disgrace, and give our next generations good reason to continue on.

Works included in this volume, or versions thereof, have been published as follows:

"Allen Ginsberg Comments on Joe Hipp, 1994" lead poem recorded for intro: Joe Hipp "The Boss" Tribute, First Northern Plains Heavyweight Champion Poetry Bout, High Plains Bookfest, Billings, Montana, 2004. Contenders: Henry Real Bird and Luke Warm Water. This poem is a tribute to Allen Ginsberg's "Howl" and other works.

"Self-Immolation" from *Rock, Ghost, Willow, Deer*, (University of Nebraska Press Bison Books American Indian Lives Series) 2004.

"Wachovia Wilds" in *North Carolina Literary Review*, (Greenville, NC) 2004.

"Voucher, Voucher" in *Cream City Review*, Karen Auvinen, ed. (Milwaukee, WI) 2003.

"Street Confetti" and "Eternity Safeway" on *Xcp: Streetnotes Online Literary Magazine*, David Michalski, ed. (Davis, CA) 2003.

"Packin' Four Corner Nabs" in *Xcp: Cross Cultural Poetics*, #9 "Writing (Working) Class." College of St. Catherine, Mark Nowak, ed. (Minneapolis, MN) 2001.

"Putting Up Beans" in *The Iowa Review*, special edition of Native American writers from the Institute of American Indian Arts, University of Iowa, Arthur Sze and Jon Davis, ed. (Iowa) 2001.

"Sorrel Run" in *The South Dakota Review*, Native American Issue. University of South Dakota, Brian Bedard, ed. (Vermillion, South Dakota) 2000.

"Off-Season" in *The World* (number 54, The Poetry Project, St. Mark's Church), Ed Friedman, ed. (New York) 1998.

"Annular Eclipse" in *Phoenix*, Susan Semrow, ed. (Tahlequah, OK) 1998.

"A White Lady Speaks" in *Phatitude*, (New Jersey) 1997.

"Baggage" in *the eleventh muse*, John Theylin, ed. (Colorado Springs) 1996.

"#4 Southwest Chief/L.A. Central" and "The Dove" in *The Santa Barbara Review*, Patricia Stockton Leddy, ed. (Santa Barbara, CA) 1996.

"Wheat" in *Listen to the Wild*, (San Francisco, CA: California Poets in the Schools Press) 1996.

"Red Stone Panther" in *Tree in the Sky*, (San Francisco, CA: California Poets in the Schools Press) 1995.

"Resonance in Motion" in *Gatherings*, (Penticton, British Columbia, Canada: Theytus Books/Enow'kin Centre) 1993.

"Casting Vessel" in *It's Not Quiet Anymore*, (Sante Fe, NM: Institute of American Indian Arts) 1993.

"The Change" in *Caliban*, (Lawrence, Long Beach, CA) 1992, in *Reinventing the Enemy's Language*, (Norton, 1997), and from *Dog Road Woman*, Coffee House Press, 1997.

Colophon

Off-Season City Pipe was designed at Coffee House Press
in the Warehouse District of downtown Minneapolis.
Poems are set in Kinesis; titles in Skia.

Funder Acknowledgments

Coffee House Press is an independent nonprofit literary publisher. Our books are made possible through the generous support of grants and gifts from many foundations, corporate giving programs, individuals, and through state and federal support. Coffee House Press receives general operating support from the Minnesota State Arts Board, through an appropriation by the Minnesota State Legislature and from the National Endowment for the Arts, a federal agency. Coffee House receives major funding from the McKnight Foundation, and from Target. Coffee House also receives significant support from: an anonymous donor; the Buuck Family Foundation; the Bush Foundation; the Patrick and Aimee Butler Family Foundation; Consortium Book Sales and Distribution; the Foundation for Contemporary Performance Art; Stephen and Isabel Keating; the Lerner Family Foundation; the Outagamie Foundation; the Pacific Foundation; the law firm of Schwegman, Lundberg, Woessner & Kluth, P.A.; the James R. Thorpe Foundation; West Group; the Woessner Freeman Family Foundation; and many other generous individual donors.

This activity is made possible in part by a grant from the Minnesota State Arts Board, through an appropriation by the Minnesota State Legislature and a grant from the National Endowment for the Arts.

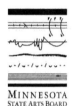
MINNESOTA
STATE ARTS BOARD

NATIONAL
ENDOWMENT
FOR THE ARTS

To you and our many readers across the country,
we send our thanks for your continuing support.

Good books are brewing at coffeehousepress.org